TO KEEP TIME

ALSO BY JOSEPH MASSEY

FULL-LENGTH BOOKS:

Areas of Fog (Shearsman Books, 2009)
At the Point (Shearsman Books, 2011)

CHAPBOOKS:

Minima St. (Range, 2002)
Eureka Slough (Effing Press, 2005)
Bramble (Hot Whiskey, 2005)
Property Line (Fewer & Further Press, 2006)
November Graph (Longhouse, 2007)
Within Hours (The Fault Line Press, 2008)
Out of Light (Kitchen Press, 2008)
The Lack Of (Nasturtium Press, 2009)
Mock Orange (Longhouse, 2010)
Exit North (Book Thug, 2010)
Another Rehearsal for Morning (Longhouse, 2012)
Thaw Compass (PressBoardPress, 2013)
An Interim (Tungsten Press, 2014)

TO KEEP TIME

+

JOSEPH MASSEY

Cover art by Wendy Heldmann. Courtesy of the artist.

Cover and interior design by James Meetze.

Offset printed in the United States
by Edwards Brothers Malloy, Ann Arbor, Michigan
On 55# Enviro Natural 100% Recycled 100% PCW
Acid Free Archival Quality FSC Certified Paper
with Rainbow FSC Certified Colored End Papers

Library of Congress Cataloging-in-Publication Data

Massey, Joseph.
  [Poems. Selections]
  To keep time / Joseph Massey.
    pages cm
  ISBN 978-1-890650-97-1 (pbk. : alk. paper)
  I. Title.
  PS3613.A81933T63 2014
  811'.6--dc23
                                        2014013753

Published by Omnidawn Publishing, Richmond, California
www.omnidawn.com (510) 237-5472 (800) 792-4957
10 9 8 7 6 5 4 3 2 1
ISBN: 978-1-890650-97-1

CONTENTS

ANOTHER REHEARSAL FOR MORNING 9

AN UNDISCLOSED LOCATION IN NORTHERN
CALIFORNIA 13

DROWSE 20

THE BLOCK 23

RECEIPT 24

FIRST THING 25

APPROACH 26

THE SEAMS 31

SURROUND 35

THE CELL (END OF NOVEMBER) 36

PASSAGE 37

OTHER INCREMENTS 38

ANCHORITIC 39

LAST MEASURE 40

MICROCLIMATE(S) 43

VAULT 57

CLOSE ENOUGH 60

THE BEND 63

VERNAL EQUINOX 67

GONE 75

THE PENINSULA 76

WRACK ZONE 77

BOOK 79

FENCED 80

TRANSIENT 81

ROOST 82

NAMES 85

NOTES 87

ACKNOWLEDGMENTS 89

The names get us through
the days

which is not enough and too much.

—John Taggart

repetition, change:
a continuity, the what
of which you are a part.

—James Schuyler

Beyond a hand
held beyond itself
the mist is too thick to see.
A dream fragment (a phrase
I wanted to remember)
goes mute in this—
extinguished. Call it
consciousness. What
we lose to recover.
Acacia branches bend
the hill's edge
off-orange. A blur,
a deeper blur.
A clarity I can't carry.

Over a gorge flanked
by black oak
ravens relay calls

that double back in
echo. Thick
morning thinned to a

pitch of sun and no
hangover.
Here you're either lost

or lost. A wordless-
ness written
into the dirt writes

itself around you.

+

Wire-mesh fence—from
this angle—
quarters the day-lit

quarter moon.

+

As long as blood runs
the body,
there is no silence.

Silence hums. A sound.
The sound of
next to nothing—no-

thing—under our skin.

+

Parenthetical
pampas grass
shrouds a used condom

in useless shadow.

+

Information plaque
words worn to
glyphs. Jagged weather—

gouged-out cliff ledge clutched
by bramble-
fused shrubs. Vertigo

holds my body here.

+

A fog bank fastens
horizon
to horizon. Names

unfold the field. My
mind is lapped
and lost in it. Lapped

and lost in this slow
flowering
of form flowering

out of form.

+

World no more a world
than thinking
allows, and the light

bound here in its place.

Space heater hum
displaces rain

as tonight's
accompaniment

to silence. What
counts for it

when even
breathing's a

sound, skunks
scuffle under

the floorboards
and a car alarm's

echo comes apart
in a parking lot.

To keep time—
to keep time by—

interstices
splint the dark.

+

First sun all month
throws the room off-

center. A nausea-
inducing blue

subsumes the window.
Power lines

suspend a crow—

sliver of cellophane
cinched in its beak

reflects sun
after a month of

low ceilings, rain

and sirens sealing

the hours shut.

+

On scintillated
pavement

shadows

segment.

Inward
a world

accumulates.

No change beyond air
smelling faintly of old piss.
A neon liquor store sign
strains to break the overcast.
How November moves.
Stunted palm tree's
stunted shadow sutures
curb to street, street to
curb—to lawn glazed
white with television. I
walk, watch day dissolve
on waking's edge—
those impossible lines
consciousness repels.

RECEIPT

Wall streaked
of soot of

moths crushed
months ago

as dawn closes
in, opening
the room.

To wait

for what
the weather's
saying

to lay
the day
unnameable.

Day collects
object by object
under puzzled over-
cast. What wakes
when waking. Patterns
animate walls, blind
corners, curbs.
Obstructions clear
a path to think
while the real flares
in and out of focus.
Vacillation voices
a world. We stand,
somehow, in place.

APPROACH

There's room
in the room
for you
to not
think in.

All autumn—
the rot of it.

+

What I
want to
remember, No-

vember forgets.
Cold con-
centrates

vacancy.

+

Things remain—won't
budge—no matter

what we say
(day, night)

to get
through.

+

Clouds—no,
cloud—
a seamless dome

stilted
by a telephone pole.

+

Sideways rain
and a lamp on
in the middle of the afternoon.

Listen to the walls.

Listen to the room
turn
inside out.

THE SEAMS

Sun gluts a gull's
syllable lodged in fog.

+

Leaves and
litter lashed
wet against
     roots

knuckled at
the sidewalk's
     edge.

+

Aural under-
brush of insects

an ambulance
bores a slit through.

+

Only this
much room

left on
the page   dusk

pools over.

SURROUND

Three weeks of rain.
The wreckage glitters.

A cold front culls other colors: look
long enough and the brush becomes
another hill or mountain, cloud

crowding skyline.
The mind

brought past its racket
swallows each gradation.

A private speech, a season.

Along lines of dust
suspended in
dust, sun divides

the room, while
wind trades
texture with talk

radio static; and the
occasional crow's
throat-thrown

consonant, how it
slips through.
The noise,

the sleight
of day—
company.

Cold, yet
the page radiates
with what night can't condense.
Call it

winter, this
wracked interior
no light lifts.
Hail,

a sudden
gust, throttles
the roof
as if to describe it.

Winter's arrhythmic timbre
dislocates landscape, con-
jures robins where frost

and mud would be.
This supposed January.
No rain to fail to say

the hours through: the din,
the dumb show, the light
off-kilter and hollowing.

How everyday ready-mades
anchor the real. Acacia
blooms—migraine yellow—

approach the window.
Turn. Find tide's out:
black plane beneath water's

holographic gray.
Cloud rifts rove.
Three bees drone

around the sill
as if to carve their form
from warped wood.

ANCHORITIC

Listening to wind
dislodge objects
in the dark around
my room, I want
to think thinking
is enough to locate
a world, but it isn't.
It isn't this one.
It isn't this world,
weather.

No knowing whether
night or day, day
or dusk.

Black in-
grown white—light
leaching light.

There's a sky: a surface

warbling: heat
or water.

And there:
an impression
pressed shallow
in muddled
scrub.

The imagination
craves a ghost.

MICROCLIMATE(S)

Ecstasy evolves slowly
within
a closed horizon

—Pam Rehm

Place,
placed apart.

Sun scrapes hills—
an outline

wedged in
white, off-white.

(The limits
delineate particulars.)

Tide gone
out, shore

pocked, mud
balked with debris.

Weeds saturated black
tangle between

barnacle-
crusted pylons.

The near silence
rattles me

to attention.
Nest of stone

foam slaps.
Something

lifts, settles
on the water:

a name,
a nonsense syllable.

+

The air itself dismantled
thread by braided
thread.

      Shadows fall farther
from what they fail to copy.

I squint
to hear the ocean
pierce an aperture
in sky

not wide enough
for words—

even *a* word—
to escape.

+

No time to think
or speak when sky
cleaves rain and sun
filtered through stacked
clouds, a kind of kaleidoscope
you can't imagine as California
imagines it: the scale
disrupts the ordinary borders:
edges the eye holds to
flake off in shade
wavering   as an eddy.

A vividness
leaves you beside yourself.

+

Rain stops, things
shattered
mend.

A split minute
of blindness
before objects
take shape.
Field's
furrowed
gradations

no palette
or pixel
could conjure.
And now wind

picks up,
snagging
the glare—

the glare
snagging
wind.

+

Season signaled by webs

clasped or partial-
ly clasped to
shadowed gaps

visible
when a thread's glint
grips an eye and

captures how round the sun

cuts
between houses.

+

Bewilder-
ment persists
in this persistent
pressure gradient.
What I want to say
I can't see to say

I can't see to say it.

Hills twine power lines
now that the sky cracks
to let some-
thing other than

its own
involution
through.

+

Ripped thin stratus
—a false horizon.

No room for music
when weather walls thought.

To find a way to live
with the gray—
is the thing. To walk
without rut or ledge; to track

through static. To stop looking
as if looking
were a way out.

+

Thorns hitch
half-spun web to half-
spun web
        where brush
twisted into itself
twists outward, filters
shadow through vines:

patterns on
        shed metal
track time.

+

All white,
white, green

and a lamp
at the center

suspends amber
where hills

slip
dusk.

+

Dryer-vent steam
veils hydrangeas

in the driveway.
A rat runs under

the house.

+

Animal noise
boils over
and sky spools up

sloughed off
marine layer

to pronounce *a* world
at once

found as it is
given.

VAULT

The invisible
world

is the visible
world.

Eucalyptus limbs'
leaves

fill and empty
wind.

+

Metal shed
roof reflects treetop
geometry—blinds me.

+

Faster than thought
a hummingbird flashes

out of frame,

frantic
in the cold.

Encaustic cumulus roves
over the momentary
world's
momentary parts.

Sun glosses
frost on the lawn.

+

Weather's
            rhythms hinge
to each color
                cloud-cut
                open.

+

In the time it takes
for a thought

to think itself
wordless   haze

wraps halfway
around a mountain.

THE BEND

Mosquitoes
entwine,

synchronized,

above a sidewalk
blistered

with bird shit.

+

Low clouds shear the hills in half.

+

Not quite a false spring.

A glow
gnaws the boundaries—

+

light

bleeding

various

invasives.

Distant shit
and wet moss

laced through
what winter's

left: radiated

rain, warped
windowsill,

wind-seething
eucalyptus.

+

Ocean-shoved
cumulus cloud

incises horizon

held by hills
and radio towers'

red, volleyed lights.

+

As if to pin
a thought

to the back
of my skull

  a humming-
bird pivots,
peers

through me
—its red-

metallic
throat a-

float
in fog.

+
.

Bracken-
thick

shade

lichen

alights.

+

From all corners

stars confuse the dark.
Compound the dark.

Frogs chant in tandem

over a seasonal creek's
flat, static whisk.

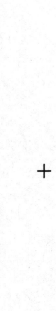

GONE

Some evidence
of a world
raw to my waking, word-

     less at first, re-
coils into noise—

Name it summer,

an after-
thought,
a hangover.

A monkey flower

           flung
over its own shadow.

Caught up
in a susurrant
fluctuation of

water,
water wringing out
air—the Pacific

as it
pares down a presumed
soundlessness: a breath

at the
center of the room
dislodged by a word

distinct
from traffic: sustained
and refracted through

dunes and
dolosse—to notice
there is nothing to

notice
beyond the weight of
what there is to hear.

It's the ocean
sounding out

a panic
I otherwise

couldn't
pronounce.

Ouroboric
vowel fixed

to a low sky's
loop of

variable white.

\+

Decayed
rope of

bull-head
kelp

distends
from tide-

tamped
sand.

Mind
mirrors

that surface,
shape,

the moment
I imagine

if I thought
far enough

I'd leave my
face.

Impossible to
read, the glare
at once bright and faint.

Haze incandescent,
compressed by
heat colliding with

the marine layer.
July has
no memory. No-

thing's retained, the land-
scape shape-shifts
continually

and there is no ground
for the mind
to stand on, to sense

itself here. This un-
remittent
elsewhere, at once too

bright, too faint to read.

FENCED

The day is
contrapuntal:

dogs bark,
vehicles
plunk past.

In air gritty
with ocean

horseflies
and gnats

etch
colliding
hieroglyphs

while the
humming-
bird feeder

sways in time
to a thought

interrupted,
moment-

arily empty.

TRANSIENT

At the end of a path
in a westernmost city
some sprawling pastel plant
I still don't know the name of

wilts over an oval stone.
Fog from the coast

blue as a vein.
Tree-frog jabber
thins thicket-dense shade.

Just enough—

enough static
to confuse things into place.

Confusion under eaves
unknown calls
before dusk
on the cusp the clangor
vivifies dulled
dulling sun what
doesn't the mind mangle
weather revolves
above the peninsula
consumes it
and my vision   there
is no other world.

and what remains of them. Night,
here, coheres;
and the mind unsettles in.

The first section of "Microlimate(s)" is a response to—and takes a few words from—Thomas A. Clark's *Creag Liath.*

"Another Rehearsal for Morning" is dedicated to Lorine Niedecker ("I carry / my clarity / with me").

"Last Measure" is a response to Sally Mann's series of Civil War battlefield photographs by the same title.

ACKNOWLEDGMENTS

Some of these poems—often in different versions—first appeared in *14 Magazine, BPM, The Brooklyn Rail, The Cultural Society, Everyday Genius, Free Verse, The Laurel Review, L'usage, Manor House Quarterly, Map Literary, Ping Pong, Poets.org, South Dakota Review, Stolen Island,* and *Western Humanities Review.*

A handful of these poems were published as an accordion-style booklet from Longhouse Books under the title *Another Rehearsal for Morning.*

"Approach," "Surround," and "Vault" were published as limited-edition broadsides from Tungsten Press.

My gratitude to the editors.

Thanks also to Steven Fama, Andrew Mister, Anthony Robinson, Jess Mynes, Peter Gizzi, Pam Rehm, Mary Austin Speaker, Lynn Melnick, Ashley Capps, Craig Dworkin, Kathy Glass, Scott Holmquist, Sara Mumolo, Joyce Yowell, and Floyd, for their support during the composition of these poems.

Joseph Massey is the author of *Areas of Fog* (Shearsman Books, 2009) and *At the Point* (Shearsman Books, 2011), as well as thirteen chapbooks. He lives in the Pioneer Valley of Massachusetts.

TO KEEP TIME

JOSEPH MASSEY

Cover art by Wendy Heldmann. Courtesy of the artist.

Cover and interior design by James Meetze.

Offset printed in the United States
by Edwards Brothers Malloy, Ann Arbor, Michigan
On 55# Enviro Natural 100% Recycled 100% PCW
Acid Free Archival Quality FSC Certified Paper
with Rainbow FSC Certified Colored End Papers

Omnidawn Publishing
Richmond, California
2014

Rusty Morrison & Ken Keegan, Senior Editors & Publishers
Gillian Hamel, Managing Poetry Editor & OmniVerse Managing Editor
Cassandra Smith, Poetry Editor & Book Designer
Peter Burghardt, Poetry Editor & Book Designer
Turner Canty, Poetry Editor
Liza Flum, Poetry Editor & Social Media
Sharon Osmond, Poetry Editor & Bookstore Outreach
Pepper Luboff, Poetry Editor & Feature Writer
Juliana Paslay, Fiction Editor & Bookstore Outreach Manager
Gail Aronson, Fiction Editor
RJ Ingram, Social Media
Melissa Burke, Poetry Editor & Feature Writer
Sharon Zetter, Grant Writer & Poetry Editor